FIND 10 CHANGES AND KEEP RECORD ■■■■■■■■■ Ans: on page # 101

FIND 10 CHANGES AND KEEP RECORD ■ ■ ■ ■ ■ ■ ■ ■ □ □ □

PUZZLE # 4

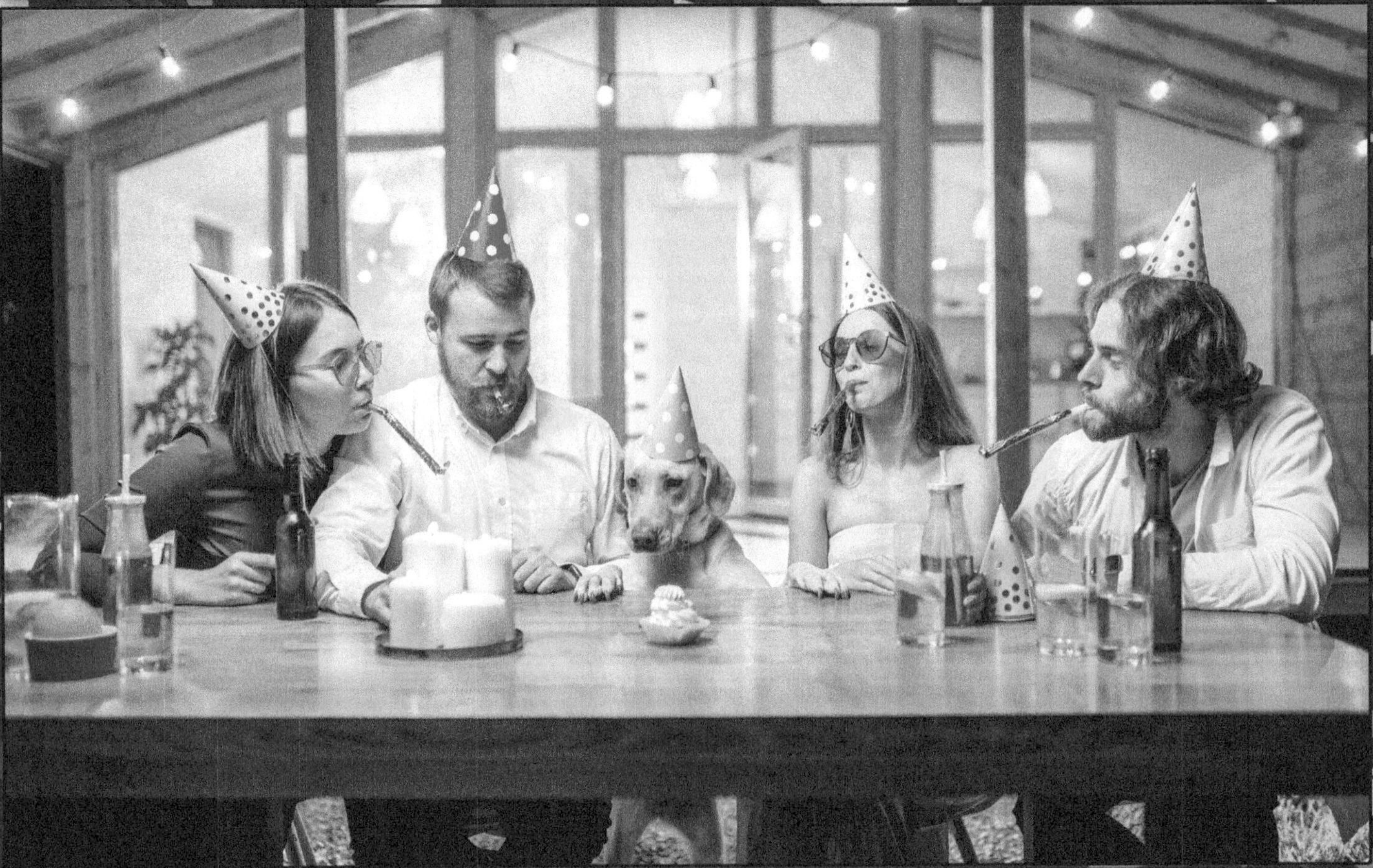

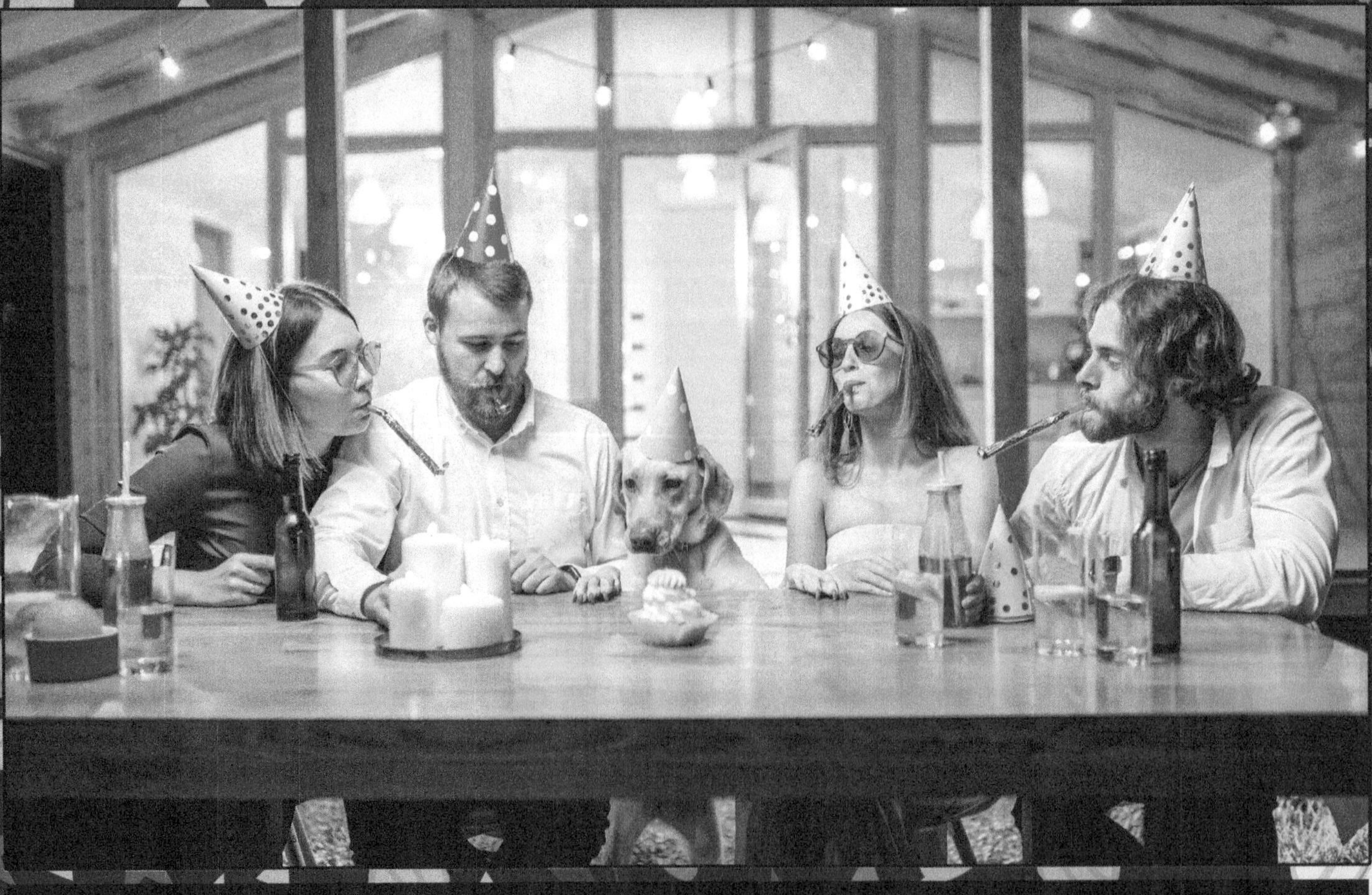

FIND 10 CHANGES AND KEEP RECORD ■■■■■■■■■■

Ans: on page # 101

FIND 10 CHANGES AND KEEP RECORD ■■■■■■■■■■ Ans: on page # 101

PUZZLE # 10

FIND 10 CHANGES AND KEEP RECORD ■■■■■■■■■

HAPPY BIRTH DAY

PUZZLE # 12

FIND 10 CHANGES AND KEEP RECORD ■■■■■■■■■■■

PUZZLE # 14

FIND 10 CHANGES AND KEEP RECORD ■■■■■■■■■■

FIND 10 CHANGES AND KEEP RECORD ■ ■ ■ ■ ■ ■ ■ ■ □ □ Ans: on page # 103

FIND 10 CHANGES AND KEEP RECORD ■ ■ ■ ■ ■ ■ ■ ■ ■ ■ Ans: on page # 104

PUZZLE # 28

FIND 10 CHANGES AND KEEP RECORD ■■■■■■■■■□□□

FIND 10 CHANGES AND KEEP RECORD ■■■■■■■□□□□

FIND 10 CHANGES AND KEEP RECORD ■■■■■■■■■■ Ans: on page # 106

FIND 10 CHANGES AND KEEP RECORD ■■■■■■■■■■■■■ Ans: on page # 106

FIND 10 CHANGES AND KEEP RECORD ▪▪▪▪▪▪▪▪▪▪▪▪ Ans: on page # 106

PUZZLE # 50

FIND 10 CHANGES AND KEEP RECORD ■ ■ ■ ■ ■ ■ ■ ■ ■ ■ Ans: on page # 107

FIND 10 CHANGES AND KEEP RECORD ■■■■■■■■■■ Ans: on page # 107

FIND 10 CHANGES AND KEEP RECORD ■■■■■■■■■■ Ans: on page # 108

FIND 10 CHANGES AND KEEP RECORD ■■■■■■■■■■□□ Ans: on page # 108

PUZZLE # 64

FIND 10 CHANGES AND KEEP RECORD ■■■■■■■■■■ Ans: on page # 109

FIND 10 CHANGES AND KEEP RECORD ■■■■■■■■■■■■ Ans: on page # 109

FIND 10 CHANGES AND KEEP RECORD ■■■■■■■■■■■■ Ans: on page # 110

PUZZLE # 84

FIND 10 CHANGES AND KEEP RECORD ■■■■■■■■■■■■ Ans: on page # 111

PUZZLE # 88

FIND 10 CHANGES AND KEEP RECORD ■ ■ ■ ■ ■ ■ ■ ■ ■ ■ Ans: on page # 111

FIND 10 CHANGES AND KEEP RECORD ▪▪▪▪▪▪▪▪▪▫▫▫ Ans: on page # 112

FIND 10 CHANGES AND KEEP RECORD ■■■■■■■■■■■■ Ans: on page # 113

FIND 10 CHANGES AND KEEP RECORD ■■■■■■■■■■■ Ans: on page # 113

A REQUEST!

CAN WE EXPECT AN EXCELLENT REVIEW FOR THIS WORK? PRODUCING THESE BOOKS ARE VERY DIFFICULT AND TIME CONSUMING. WE WILL APPRECIATE IF YOU WRITE A POSITIVE REVIEW ON AMAZON. BEST WISHES FOR YOU!